A HAGGADAH
FOR FAMILIES

✳ ✳ ✳ ✳ ✳ ✳ ✳ ✳ ✳✳ ✳ ✳ ✳✳ ✳

"In every generation we should see ourselves
as if we personally came out of Egypt."

✳ ✳ ✳ ✳ ✳✳ ✳ ✳ ✳ ✳✳ ✳ ✳ ✳✳ ✳

The Passover **seder**, the traditional meal and celebration for Passover, is designed to be an experience that everyone can share — adults and children. It includes stories, questions, explanations, special foods, and even a game of hide-and-seek. The **Haggadah**, the traditional guidebook to this special night, includes a reminder that on the seder night, everyone should be welcome at our table. The story of freedom is made for sharing.

This Haggadah is designed to help families with young children enjoy a Passover seder together. All of the core elements of a seder are included, in a form that is shortened and explained to make it easy for everyone to participate — even if it is their first seder.

WHAT'S IN THIS BOOK?

Seder means "order." Even a simple Haggadah includes many different blessings, songs, and stories that take place in a traditional order. This Haggadah helps families keep track of their progress by dividing the seder into five sections:

 Welcome: This section sets the scene for the start of the seder.

 First Steps: This section starts with the chanting of the steps of the seder. It includes the *kiddush* blessings said over our first cup of wine and other rituals that get us ready to tell our freedom story.

 The Story of Freedom: The longest section of the seder is called *Magid*, which means "tell." In this section we tell, sing, act, and ask questions about the Passover story from many different angles.

 A Special Meal: We start our seder dinner with blessings over the second cup of wine and other special foods, and we end it with thanks for what we have eaten and blessings over our third cup.

 Celebrate!: This section includes songs of joy and gratitude. Along with the fourth and final cup of wine, it concludes our seder.

Each section includes key blessings, songs, and other passages from the traditional text in Hebrew and in transliteration (Hebrew words printed in English letters) with clear English translations. Combine the explanations, Hebrew, and English in any way that works for your seder.

YOUR HAGGADAH KEY

Look for these symbols throughout the Haggadah.

? QUESTIONS TO ASK AND DISCUSS AT YOUR TABLE

WAYS TO ACT OUT THE PASSOVER STORY

SONGS TO SING OUT LOUD

It helps to have a leader direct activities and keep the evening moving smoothly.

CUSTOMIZE YOUR SEDER

≪ ≫ ≪ ≫ ≪ ≫ ≪ ≫ ≪ ≫ ≪ ≫ ≪

Customizing your seder is an important part of the experience. While creativity and surprise help us feel free — a good Passover feeling — planning some of your seder elements in advance will make the evening more fun and meaningful.

- **Decorate.** A special cup for wine, a decorated cloth to wrap the matzah, and placemats with drawings from the Passover story can make setting the table feel more special and build anticipation. Preparing them can give kids a role in getting ready, too.

- **Add drama.** Bring costumes or props to the table to encourage both adults and kids to get into the act.

- **Bring your own stories.** Do any friends or family members have a freedom story to tell? Bring images or objects from their experience to help show how "in every generation" we experience the journey to freedom. Consider inviting others to prepare some of these ahead of time too.

- **Snacks for all ages.** Consider extending *karpas* (the vegetable appetizer dipped in salt water near the beginning of the seder) with extra vegetables and dips. Staving off hunger makes it easier to tell stories and ask questions until dinnertime. Just wait on eating matzah until its special moment arrives!

- **Connect to the present.** Learning about other people who have reached freedom in our own time, or who are still not free today, can help adults and kids understand the meaning of Passover.

- **Sing out!** Freedom songs in any language your family knows can enrich the Celebrate! section of the seder.

≪ ≫ ≪ ≫ ≪ ≫ ≪ ≫ ≪ ≪ ≫ ≪ ≫ ≪ ≫ ≪ ≫ ≪

Visit PJLibrary.org/passover for videos and music to prepare for your seder. You can also find suggestions for an unabridged Haggadah that you can use in combination with this one, if you have different ages or levels of interest in your group.

≪ ≫ ≪ ≫ ≪ ≫ ≪ ≫ ≪ ≪ ≫ ≪ ≫ ≪ ≫ ≪ ≫ ≪

PRE-SEDER CHECKLIST

- ☐ Wine for adults and grape juice for children (p.13)

- ☐ Seder plate with:
    - Karpas - green herb or vegetable, such as parsley (p.17)
    - Z'roa - roasted lamb shank bone (p.43)
    - Maror - horseradish or similar bitter vegetable (p.51)
    - Charoset - mixture of chopped fruits, nuts, and spices (p.52)
    - Chazeret - bitter vegetable, often romaine lettuce (p.51)
    - Beitza - roasted egg (p.53)
    - Salt water (p.17)

- ☐ Matzah - flat cracker bread that is a core Passover food (p.22)

- ☐ Plate or cloth pocket to wrap three pieces of matzah (p.18)

- ☐ Afikoman bag - pouch for hiding the special dessert matzah (p.18)

- ☐ Fun rewards - for children who find the Afikoman (p.54)

- ☐ Elijah's cup and Miriam's cup for special ceremonies (p.60)

- ☐ Cushions to recline on as a sign of freedom (p.15)

- ☐ Festive main meal (p.53)

5

THE SEDER PLATE

The foods we eat tonight help tell the story of liberation from slavery. Items on the seder plate are reminders of things like the tears of slaves and the mortar for bricks used to build pyramids. We will talk more about these symbols during the seder.

Chazeret, bitter vegetable, often romaine lettuce

EGG AND GREENERY, SYMBOLS OF SPRING AND HOPE.

Beitza, roasted egg

Charoset, sweet mortar-like mixture made of chopped fruit, nuts, spices, and wine

Salt water

Karpas, green herb or vegetable, such as parsley

Z'roa, roasted lamb shank bone

(some vegetarian families use a beet)

Maror, horseradish or similar bitter vegetable

WELCOME

TONIGHT WE CELEBRATE THE HOLIDAY OF PASSOVER.

At dinner tables around the world, families sit together to tell the story of how the Jewish people went free from slavery in Egypt.

The seder is a meal at which people sing, ask questions, and tell stories. Some of the stories are from the Torah, the first five books of the Bible, that tell about the beginnings of the Jewish people.

At the seder, we travel back in time to ancient Egypt. Our guide for the journey is this **Haggadah (hah-gah-DAH), which means "telling" in Hebrew.** Telling the Passover story helps us feel that we ourselves are going free from slavery tonight.

To set the scene, we light candles and bless the children.

Light the candles and say the blessing.

·✳·✳·✳·✳·✳·✳·✳·✳

LIGHTING THE HOLIDAY CANDLES

Jewish holidays begin at sunset with candle lighting. As darkness fills the evening sky, burning candles spark brightness inside. The candles' warm light stands for hope and freedom. On the first night of Passover, an extra blessing is added to remember how special it is to celebrate a seder for the first time in a year — or even for the first time ever.

Here is how to say the Hebrew blessing.

בָּרוּךְ אַתָּה יְיָ אֱלֹהֵינוּ מֶלֶךְ הָעוֹלָם אֲשֶׁר קִדְּשָׁנוּ בְּמִצְוֹתָיו וְצִוָּנוּ לְהַדְלִיק נֵר שֶׁל (שַׁבָּת וְשֶׁל) יוֹם טוֹב.

Baruch ata Adonai, Eloheinu melech ha'olam, asher kideshanu bemitzvotav vetzivanu lehadlik ner shel (Shabbat veshel) yom tov.

Dear God, Creator of our world, thank You for giving us rules that make our lives special and for teaching us to light these holiday candles.

✳·✳·✳·✳·✳·✳·✳·✳·

On the first night of Passover, add an extra blessing.

בָּרוּךְ אַתָּה יְיָ אֱלֹהֵינוּ מֶלֶךְ הָעוֹלָם שֶׁהֶחֱיָנוּ וְקִיְּמָנוּ וְהִגִּיעָנוּ לַזְּמַן הַזֶּה.

Baruch ata Adonai, Eloheinu melech ha'olam, shehecheyanu vekiyemanu vehigi'anu lazman hazeh.

Dear God, Creator of our world, thank You for keeping us alive so we can celebrate this important moment.

9

BLESSING THE CHILDREN

After lighting the candles, parents bless their children. The Torah recounts how Jacob blessed his grandchildren who grew up in Egypt. While they lived there, Jacob's family grew so big that it became a whole nation. That is how the Passover story begins. The children at this seder are growing, too. One day they will be grown up and may lead their own seders.

Adults place hands on children's heads and recite the blessing below:

יְבָרֶכְךָ יְיָ וְיִשְׁמְרֶךָ.
יָאֵר יְיָ פָּנָיו אֵלֶיךָ וִיחֻנֶּךָּ.
יִשָּׂא יְיָ פָּנָיו אֵלֶיךָ וְיָשֵׂם לְךָ שָׁלוֹם.

Yevarechecha Adonai veyishmerecha.
Ya'er Adonai panav eilecha viyechuneka.
Yisa Adonai panav eilecha veyasem lecha shalom.

May God bless you and keep you safe.
May God's light shine on you and grace your life.
May God turn toward you and give you a world of peace.

FIRST STEPS

WE'RE READY TO BEGIN OUR SEDER.

Together we will taste the bitterness of slavery and the joy of freedom. All of the foods, rituals, and blessings we are about to say remind us that what makes tonight special is our freedom story.

First, we'll read aloud a list of all the steps of the Passover seder. Then a special drink and snack will begin our journey back in time to when we were slaves in Egypt.

SEDER MEANS "ORDER"

Hold up the seder plate or point to it.

At the seder, we do 15 activities in a certain order. Some take only a minute to do, while others include many things to read, talk about, or sing. Reciting the 15 steps of the seder lays out the order of the seder, like a program at a play or a menu at a meal.

Read each step of the seder out loud.

Kadesh (First wine blessing) קַדֵּשׁ

Urchatz (First hand-washing) וּרְחַץ

Karpas (Eating the green vegetable with salt water) כַּרְפַּס

Yachatz (Breaking off the dessert matzah) יַחַץ

 MAGID (Telling the Passover story) מַגִּיד

Hey, let's talk about this. Discussion time!

Rachtzah (Second hand-washing) רָחְצָה

Motzi (Blessing before eating) מוֹצִיא

? PAGE **30**

Matzah (Blessing for matzah) מַצָּה

Do you like to act? Get ready for drama on PAGE **38**

Maror (Eating the bitter vegetable) מָרוֹר

Korech (Eating the matzah sandwich) כּוֹרֵךְ

SHULCHAN ORECH (Main meal) שֻׁלְחָן עוֹרֵךְ

Tzafun (Finding and eating the dessert matzah) צָפוּן

Barech (Blessing after eating) בָּרֵךְ

Hallel (Singing praise songs) הַלֵּל

Shulchan Orech? Does that mean we can eat?

NIRTZAH (Songs to finish our seder) נִרְצָה

PAGE **53**

PAGE **68** Let's sing together!

KADESH קַדֵּשׁ
First Cup of Wine

Four times during the seder we raise our cup of wine or grape juice and say a blessing before we drink it. Wine and its blessing mark special celebrations when we feel glad and grateful for good things that have happened to us. The seder is an extra special one of those nights.

The first cup of wine is called **Kadesh (kah-DESH), which means "make it holy" or "make it special"** in Hebrew. With this first cup, we add blessings that describe Passover as a gift—a time to thank God and to celebrate being free.

TONIGHT YOU ARE FREE, so let someone else fill your glass. After you say the blessings, sit down, lean back, and relax when you drink! Having someone serve you and relaxing at a meal are both privileges slaves do not enjoy.

Hold your glass with wine or grape juice and say the blessing on the next page.

בָּרוּךְ אַתָּה יְיָ אֱלֹהֵינוּ מֶלֶךְ הָעוֹלָם
בּוֹרֵא פְּרִי הַגָּפֶן.

**Baruch ata Adonai, Eloheinu melech
ha'olam, borei peri hagafen.**

Dear God, Creator of our world,
thank You for the delicious fruit that
grows on vines.

If your seder is on Friday
night, when Shabbat
is starting, begin here
and add any words that
appear in parentheses
on the next page.

When evening and
daytime were over
on the sixth day of
Creation, the sky and
earth and everything
that lives in them were
complete. Then, on the
seventh day, God ended
all of that work by
resting. God blessed the
seventh day and made
it special, because it
was the day when God
rested from all the work
of creating the world.

Dear God, Creator of our
world, You have given all the
people in the world different ways
of living and believing. Thank You for
giving us the gift of being Jewish and
the rules and good deeds that help
make us better people. With love You
have given us holidays to be joyful. On
this Festival of Matzah, we celebrate
being free people. We remember how
You took us out of the land of Egypt
where we were slaves. Dear God, thank
You for giving the Jewish people this
special time to celebrate our freedom.

בָּרוּךְ אַתָּה יְיָ אֱלֹהֵינוּ מֶלֶךְ הָעוֹלָם אֲשֶׁר בָּחַר בָּנוּ מִכָּל עָם וְרוֹמְמָנוּ מִכָּל לָשׁוֹן וְקִדְּשָׁנוּ בְּמִצְוֹתָיו. וַתִּתֶּן לָנוּ יְיָ אֱלֹהֵינוּ בְּאַהֲבָה (שַׁבָּתוֹת לִמְנוּחָה וּ) מוֹעֲדִים לְשִׂמְחָה, חַגִּים וּזְמַנִּים לְשָׂשׂוֹן, אֶת יוֹם (הַשַּׁבָּת הַזֶּה וְאֶת יוֹם) חַג הַמַּצּוֹת הַזֶּה, זְמַן חֵרוּתֵנוּ (בְּאַהֲבָה) מִקְרָא קֹדֶשׁ, זֵכֶר לִיצִיאַת מִצְרָיִם. כִּי בָנוּ בָחַרְתָּ וְאוֹתָנוּ קִדַּשְׁתָּ מִכָּל הָעַמִּים, (וְשַׁבָּת) וּמוֹעֲדֵי קָדְשֶׁךָ (בְּאַהֲבָה וּבְרָצוֹן) בְּשִׂמְחָה וּבְשָׂשׂוֹן הִנְחַלְתָּנוּ. בָּרוּךְ אַתָּה יְיָ מְקַדֵּשׁ (הַשַּׁבָּת וְ) יִשְׂרָאֵל וְהַזְּמַנִּים.

Baruch ata Adonai, Eloheinu melech ha'olam, asher bachar banu mikol am, veromemanu mikol lashon, vekideshanu bemitzvotav. Vatiten lanu Adonai Eloheinu b'ahava (Shabbatot lim'nucha u') mo'adim lesimcha, chagim uzmanim lesason, et yom (haShabbat hazeh v'et yom) chag hamatzot hazeh, zman cheruteinu (b'ahava) mikra kodesh, zecher liyetzi'at Mitzrayim. Ki vanu vacharta v'otanu kidashta mikol ha'amim, (veShabbat) umo'adei kodshecha (b'ahava uvratzon) besimcha uv'sason hinchaltanu. Baruch ata Adonai, mekadesh (haShabbat v') Yisra'el vehazmanim.

If your seder is on Saturday night, when Shabbat is ending, add:

Dear God, Creator of the world, thank You for making each time special in its own way.

On the first night of Passover add:

בָּרוּךְ אַתָּה יְיָ אֱלֹהֵינוּ מֶלֶךְ הָעוֹלָם שֶׁהֶחֱיָנוּ וְקִיְּמָנוּ וְהִגִּיעָנוּ לַזְּמַן הַזֶּה.

Baruch ata Adonai, Eloheinu melech ha'olam, shehecheyanu vekiyemanu vehigi'anu lazman hazeh.

Dear God, Creator of our world, thank You for keeping us alive so we can celebrate this important moment.

Sit down, lean back in freedom, and drink!

15

URCHATZ
וּרְחַץ

First Hand-Washing

We wash our hands so they will be ready to do special work. During the seder we wash our hands in an unusual way, and we do it twice. This first time – washing with no blessing – is **Urchatz (oor–CHATZ), which means "...and wash!"**

Three people can help each guest wash.

- **One person** can hold a bowl.

- **A second person** can hold a pitcher with water to pour over each guest's hands, which are held over the bowl.

- **A third person** can carry a towel for drying hands.

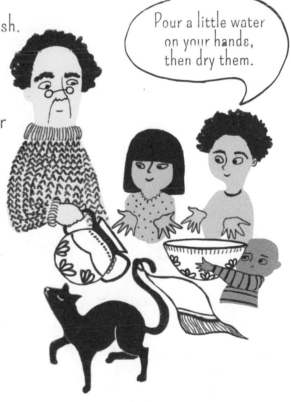

Pour a little water on your hands, then dry them.

KARPAS כַּרְפַּס
Eat a Green Vegetable Dipped in Salt Water

Passover celebrates the start of spring. As cold and dark days end, green leaves return to the trees and flowers blossom again. Trees and plants are free to grow. To mark spring's return, we eat **karpas (kar–PAHS)**, **which means "green vegetable."**
Parsley or celery can be good karpas. Before we eat the karpas, we dip it in salt water. The salty taste reminds us of the tears that the slaves cried in Egypt. It also reminds us of the sadness and pain of slavery.

Lean back in freedom and eat the salty karpas.

Dip the green vegetable in salt water, then say:

בָּרוּךְ אַתָּה יְיָ אֱלֹהֵינוּ מֶלֶךְ הָעוֹלָם בּוֹרֵא פְּרִי הָאֲדָמָה.

Baruch ata Adonai, Eloheinu melech ha'olam, borei peri ha'adama.

Dear God, Creator of our world, thank You for creating fruits and vegetables that grow out of the earth.

YACHATZ יחץ

Break off the Dessert Matzah

> Hold up the middle matzah from the ceremonial matzah plate. Break it in half. Put the smaller piece back, but wrap the larger piece in a cloth or pouch and put it aside.

The seder table has a ceremonial plate with three pieces of matzah. The middle matzah on this plate has a special job. Half of it will "hide" and come back later as the last bite of our meal. **Yachatz (yah-CHATZ) means "split in two."**

The larger piece of this matzah will be called the **Afikoman (ah-fee-koe-MAHN), an ancient Greek word that means "after-dinner fun."** In a game of hide-and-seek, adults will hide the Afikoman and children will have to find it. (In some families, the roles are reversed.)

This missing piece of matzah will be tonight's dessert. Keep a close eye on it before it disappears! At the end of the meal, you may get a prize for finding the Afikoman.

MAGID מַגִּיד

o»>———«o

THE STORY OF FREEDOM

MAKES THIS NIGHT DIFFERENT.

Magid (mah-GEED) means "tell." It is the longest part of the Haggadah, when we tell the story of how the Jewish people became slaves in Egypt and then became free. As part of the telling, we ask questions, invite discussion, and experience the story with acting and singing.

HA LACHMA ANYA

הָא לַחְמָא עַנְיָא

Matzah, the Bread of Slavery

Stand, hold up the matzah plate, and recite the section below.

הָא לַחְמָא עַנְיָא דִּי אֲכָלוּ אַבְהָתָנָא בְּאַרְעָא דְמִצְרָיִם. כָּל דִּכְפִין יֵיתֵי
וְיֵכֻל, כָּל דִּצְרִיךְ יֵיתֵי וְיִפְסַח. הָשַׁתָּא הָכָא, לְשָׁנָה הַבָּאָה בְּאַרְעָא
דְיִשְׂרָאֵל. הָשַׁתָּא עַבְדֵי, לְשָׁנָה הַבָּאָה בְּנֵי חוֹרִין.

Ha lachma anya di achalu avhatana b'ar'a deMitzrayim. Kol dichfin yeitei
v'yeichul. Kol ditzrich yeitei v'yifsach. Hashata hacha, leshana haba'a b'ar'a
d'Yisra'el. Hashata avdei, leshana haba'a benei chorin.

This is the flat, plain bread that our family ate when they were slaves in
the land of Egypt. Remembering the poor food of slaves, tonight we welcome
anyone who is hungry to come and eat the Passover meal with us. Now we are
here. Next year we hope to be in the Land of Israel. Now we are slaves.
Next year may we all be free!

WAIT, WHERE ARE WE NOW?

The Haggadah gives a clue with the words: "Now we are slaves." We are "here" in ancient Egypt. When we hold up the matzah, we imagine going back in time and becoming slaves. Now we are tired and hungry and have to eat quickly while we are forced to work.

Even though we are just beginning to tell how we became slaves, we're already getting ready to go free at the end of the story.

Refill your cup of wine or grape juice to get ready for the second cup. We will drink it later at the very end of Magid.

מצה

THE FOUR QUESTIONS
מַה נִּשְׁתַּנָּה
MA NISHTANA

Passover seders are unusual dinners, with unique foods and ways of eating. Why do we have these foods and rituals? How do they help us tell the story of having been slaves and then becoming free? Asking questions out loud and answering questions in ways that tell our own stories are both signs of being a free person.

Traditionally, the youngest person or people at the table get to ask the Four Questions.

These questions are introduced with the Hebrew phrase
Ma Nishtana (MAH neesh-tah-NAH), which means "What is different?"

מַה נִּשְׁתַּנָּה הַלַּיְלָה הַזֶּה מִכָּל הַלֵּילוֹת?

Ma nishtana halaila hazeh mikol haleilot?

Why is this night different
from all others?

1

שֶׁבְּכָל הַלֵּילוֹת אָנוּ אוֹכְלִין חָמֵץ וּמַצָּה.
הַלַּיְלָה הַזֶּה כֻּלּוֹ מַצָּה.

Shebechol haleilot, anu ochlin chametz umatzah.
Halaila hazeh, kulo matzah.

On all other nights we can eat *chametz,* bread that rises when it bakes. Why tonight do we eat only the flat bread, **matzah**?

2

שֶׁבְּכָל הַלֵּילוֹת אָנוּ אוֹכְלִין שְׁאָר יְרָקוֹת.
הַלַּיְלָה הַזֶּה מָרוֹר.

Shebechol haleilot, anu ochlin she'ar yerakot.
Halaila hazeh, maror.

On all other nights we eat any kind of vegetables. Why tonight do we eat bitter vegetables, **maror**?

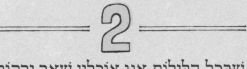

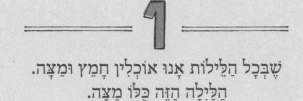

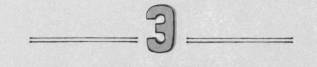

3

שֶׁבְּכָל הַלֵּילוֹת אֵין אָנוּ מַטְבִּילִין אֲפִילוּ פַּעַם אֶחָת. הַלַּיְלָה הַזֶּה שְׁתֵּי פְעָמִים.

Shebechol haleilot, ein anu matbilin afilu pa'am echat.
Halaila hazeh, shtei fe'amim.

On all other nights we don't need to dip our
food into a sauce even one time.
Why tonight do we dip foods two times?

4

שֶׁבְּכָל הַלֵּילוֹת אָנוּ אוֹכְלִין בֵּין יוֹשְׁבִין וּבֵין מְסֻבִּין. הַלַּיְלָה הַזֶּה כֻּלָּנוּ מְסֻבִּין.

Shebechol haleilot, anu ochlin bein yoshvin uvein mesubin.
Halaila hazeh, kulanu mesubin.

On all other nights we eat sitting up straight or leaning. Why tonight
do we make sure to eat leaning to our left?

QUESTIONS ARE AN IMPORTANT PART OF THE SEDER. If you think of more good questions about the activities we're doing or the story we're telling, ask them!

Tonight's seder is different from ordinary meals in all these ways because tonight is a special night. Tonight we are telling the Passover story, about how the Jewish people were slaves in Egypt and then became free.

עֲבָדִים הָיִינוּ, עַתָּה בְּנֵי חוֹרִין!

Avadim hayinu, ata benei chorin!

We were slaves, now we are free!

THE FOUR CHILDREN

חָכָם, רָשָׁע, תָּם, וְאֶחָד
שֶׁאֵינוֹ יוֹדֵעַ לִשְׁאוֹל

Chacham, rasha, tam, v'echad she'eino yode'a lish'ol

Wise, Rebellious, Simple, Quiet

In the Torah, parents tell the Passover story to their children in different ways. The Haggadah tells us that's because the children themselves are different. People learn stories in many different ways.

These four children are examples of different ways to ask and answer questions about Passover. As you read about them, try to think of other questions someone might ask about the seder and the story. What parts of the seder are you curious about?

You can also think about different ways someone might tell the story to help everyone learn it. How can food help us tell the story? How can songs help? How about pictures? What are some other ways you or other people might like to learn a story?

wise child

rebellious child

quiet child

simple child

THE WISE CHILD INQUIRES: "WHAT ARE ALL THE RULES AND CUSTOMS FOR CELEBRATING PASSOVER?"

The Wise Child wants to know all the details of everything we do and say at the seder to understand why we do and say them. What do they teach us?

Parents can explain how each of the seder's rules, customs, foods, and songs helps us tell the Passover story. On Passover, we remember our history.

THE REBELLIOUS CHILD CHALLENGES: "WHAT DOES ALL THIS MEAN TO YOU?"

The Rebellious Child feels like an outsider at the seder.

Parents can explain that the Jews in Egypt had to choose to go free all together as a community. If you did not choose to join, you would stay stuck in slavery. On Passover, when people all over the world come together to tell this story of freedom, we choose to be part of a community.

THE SIMPLE CHILD ASKS: "WHAT'S GOING ON?"

The Simple Child sees that tonight is different from other nights, but doesn't understand what we are doing or why we are doing it.

Parents can explain the reason for the seder simply: "God took Jewish slaves out of Egypt with surprising miracles." On Passover, we are grateful to be free people.

THE QUIET CHILD IS LISTENING AND THINKING AT THE SEDER, BUT NOT SPEAKING OR ASKING.

Parents can explain, even without being asked, that we celebrate Passover because God freed us from being slaves. They can invite this quiet child to keep listening and thinking. On Passover, each of us learns in our own way about being free.

THE MORE
STORYTELLING,
THE BETTER!

Now it's time to add more details to our Passover story. We will tell how we became slaves in Egypt, what it was like for us there, and then how we were liberated.

The following four verses from the Torah tell the basic story, but there is a lot for us to describe, ask, act out, and explain. On Passover, we encourage everyone to talk about this story — the more, the better!

"

OUR ANCESTORS WANDERED FROM MESOPOTAMIA. THEY TRAVELED DOWN TO EGYPT TO LIVE THERE, WITH JUST A FEW PEOPLE. THERE THEY BECAME A GREAT NATION WITH MANY, MANY PEOPLE.

"

OUR ANCESTORS WANDERED *Get up and wander!* Pick a song to sing while everyone "wanders" around the table or the room. Then go back to your seat where you feel "at home."

? **TO LIVE THERE** At first the Jews wandered from place to place, but they stopped wandering when they got to Egypt. Why did they stay there? What makes people feel at home in a new place?

? Have you ever been a stranger in a new place, or with new people? How did it feel? Did some new people make you feel welcome? Was anyone angry or mean? How did you react?

? **A GREAT NATION** First, the Jews were a family, but in Egypt they became a nation. How is a nation similar to a family? How is it different? What makes a nation "great" besides having a lot of people?

> " THE EGYPTIANS WERE HARSH TO US, AND <u>MADE US SUFFER</u>, AND FORCED US <u>TO WORK VERY HARD</u>. "

MADE US SUFFER The Torah tells that the Egyptians took children away from their parents. Moses, who led the Jews to freedom, was saved when he was a baby because his mother hid him in a basket that floated down the river.

Imagine Moses is your baby. You are so afraid that he will not be safe that you wrap him up and hide him in a basket. Show how you'll place Moses in a basket on the river. *Is it hard to let him go? Will he be OK? Who will find him? How do you feel as the basket floats away?*

WORK VERY HARD Pharaoh, the ruler of Egypt, forced the slaves to build cities and pyramids – and even make the bricks for building!

? Is it cruel to make someone work hard? What kinds of hard work are good for us, and what kinds are cruel?

Pretend you're a slave, lifting heavy bricks in the blinding sun. Your whole body aches and you're not allowed to stop. Show how it feels to be forced to work so hard. *What are you thinking to yourself as you work?*

> ❝
> ─────────────
>
> WE CALLED OUT TO GOD, WHOM OUR
> ANCESTORS HAD PRAYED TO. GOD
> HEARD OUR VOICE, AND SAW OUR PAIN,
> OUR STRUGGLE, AND OUR SUFFERING.
>
> ───────────── ❞

CALLED OUT What do you think the Jews said when they called out to God? Did they feel sad or angry, frightened or hopeful?

"Hey, God, listen!" Imagine you're a slave talking to God. *How do you describe how you feel? What would you like to say to God?*

GOD HEARD First, God heard the people's voice when they called out. Then God saw how they felt. How is hearing what someone says to us different from seeing what their life is like?

OUR SUFFERING Who in the world today is suffering and needs help? Who do we know who helps other people, and how do they do it? Are there some ways *we* could help other people, too?

"

GOD TOOK US OUT OF EGYPT, WITH A STRONG
HAND AND AN OUTSTRETCHED ARM — WITH
GREAT POWER, AND WITH SIGNS AND WONDERS.

"

 WITH A STRONG HAND What does it mean to say God did something "with a strong hand"?

 AN OUTSTRETCHED ARM Did someone ever "reach out," with their arms or their words, to help you when you needed help? How did you feel before they helped you? How did you feel afterward?

 SIGNS AND WONDERS Did you ever see something that made you feel a sense of wonder?

 Does someone at your seder table have a **FREEDOM STORY** to tell? Now is a good time to share it.

TEN PLAGUES

What were those powerful signs and wonders? We begged Pharaoh, the ruler of Egypt, to let us go free, but Pharaoh's heart was as hard as stone. To change Pharaoh's heart, God sent ten messages. Each message was a plague – something frightening or bad, that could make Pharaoh understand that what he was doing was wrong.

These Ten Plagues scared the Egyptians. Some of the plagues ruined things that Egyptians prayed to, like the Nile River and the sun. Some made them sick, like sores, or spoiled their food, like locusts that ate up the plants in the fields. After each plague, Pharaoh thought about letting the Jews go free, but he always changed his mind.

Finally, God sent the tenth – and worst – plague: the eldest son in every Egyptian family got sick and died. At last, Pharaoh said, "Enough! Let the Jews go."

On Passover, we are grateful that extraordinary things happened to help us go free. But we're also sad that other people suffered while we were saved. When we remember the Ten Plagues, we dip a pinky finger into our cup of wine or grape juice and take one drop out for each plague. We're still joyful, but our cup of joy is not quite as full.

Say the names of the Ten Plagues. Each time, use your finger to move a drop of wine or grape juice from your cup to your plate.

× ×

Blood (Dam) דָּם

Frogs (Tzefarde'a) צְפַרְדֵּעַ

Lice (Kinim) כִּנִּים

Wild Animals (Arov) עָרוֹב

Cattle Disease (Dever) דֶּבֶר

Sores (Shechin) שְׁחִין

Hail (Barad) בָּרָד

Locusts (Arbeh) אַרְבֶּה

Darkness (Choshech) חֹשֶׁךְ

Death of the Firstborn (Makat Bechorot) מַכַּת בְּכוֹרוֹת

× ×

QUICK!

Pharaoh always changes his mind about letting us go free. We have to hurry. The morning bread we are baking can't rise any longer. Throw the dough in a sack on your back. The sun will bake it into matzah. We have to run!

Act out the scene on these pages. As you read aloud the section to the left, how would you walk through the sea? Try to think of creative ways to re-enact crossing to freedom.

We are rushing away from Egypt toward the Sinai Desert. We come to the Sea of Reeds. On the other side is freedom.

Look! Pharaoh has changed his mind again. His soldiers are chasing after us, coming to drag us back to slavery. How can we get to the other side of the sea before they catch us?

But then a miracle happens. God sends a strong wind to push up the sea on both sides. We rush across between the walls of water. Just in time we make it to the other side. The walls of water crash back down, trapping the Egyptians.

For a moment everything is quiet. Then we burst into song. We are free at last!

DAYENU דַּיֵּנוּ
More than Enough for Us!

These powerful signs and wonders told the Egyptians to let us go free. They also showed us that God was listening to us and working in special ways to take us out of slavery.

Dayenu (die-AY-new) means "It is more than enough for us!" God has given the Jewish people so many gifts — and even just one of them would have been enough for us to feel grateful and happy.

It's time to sing!

אִלּוּ הוֹצִיאָנוּ מִמִּצְרַיִם: דַּיֵּנוּ!

אִלּוּ קָרַע לָנוּ אֶת הַיָּם: דַּיֵּנוּ!

אִלּוּ נָתַן לָנוּ אֶת הַשַּׁבָּת: דַּיֵּנוּ!

אִלּוּ נָתַן לָנוּ אֶת הַתּוֹרָה: דַּיֵּנוּ!

אִלּוּ הִכְנִיסָנוּ לְאֶרֶץ יִשְׂרָאֵל: דַּיֵּנוּ!

Ilu hotzi'anu miMitzrayim: dayenu!

Ilu kara lanu et hayam: dayenu!

Ilu natan lanu et haShabbat: dayenu!

Ilu natan lanu et haTorah: dayenu!

Ilu hichnisanu l'eretz Yisra'el: dayenu!

If God had only taken us out of Egypt, it would have been enough.
If God had only split the sea for us, it would have been enough.
If God had only given us Shabbat, it would have been enough.
If God had only given us the Torah, it would have been enough.
If God had only brought us into Israel, it would have been enough.

TELLING THE STORY WITH FOODS:
PESACH, MATZAH, AND MAROR

פֶּסַח, מַצָּה, וּמָרוֹר

Rabban Gamliel was a teacher who lived in Israel 2,000 years ago and who helped write the Haggadah. He wanted us to make sure that the foods at our seder are not just for eating. They are on our table to remind us what the Jews felt at the first Passover celebration, the last night of slavery.

RABBAN GAMLIEL SAID: Every Passover seder should include the story of these three items – the lamb bone, the matzah, and the maror.

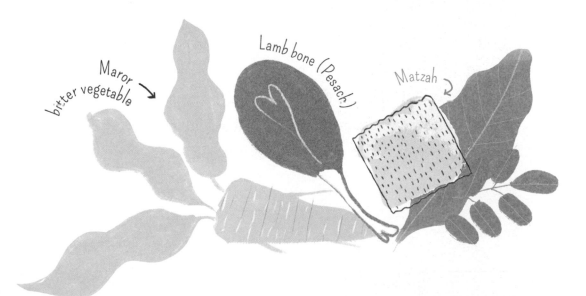

Maror
bitter vegetable

Lamb bone (Pesach)

Matzah

LAMB BONE

Point to the lamb bone on the seder plate.

This roasted lamb bone is called **Pesach (PEH-sach), the Hebrew name for the Passover holiday.** Why is it on our seder table?

On the Jews' last night as slaves in Egypt, each family shared a feast of roasted lamb. When God sent the frightening Tenth Plague to every house in Egypt, God "passed over," or skipped, the houses where Jews were getting ready to go free. The lamb was a sign to God that the Jews were choosing to go free.

The lamb bone connects us to that first Passover celebration and reminds us that we are choosing to celebrate Passover now.

MATZAH

Lift up the matzah in its cloth.

This matzah that we will eat in a few moments – why is it on our seder table?

Matzah is made of the same dough as bread, but we mix and bake it much faster. That's why it stays flat and dry. Matzah reminds us that when Pharaoh finally agreed to let us go, we had to leave Egypt fast! There was no time to get ready or to wait.

Eating matzah at the seder reminds us of slavery and also of freedom, because we took it with us to eat when we could not stay as slaves even one more hour.

MAROR

Lift up the maror from the seder plate.

This bitter vegetable is called **maror (mah-ROAR), which means "something bitter."** Why is it on our seder table?

Maror has a sharp, harsh taste. Eating the maror is supposed to sting our mouths a little. Maror's harshness reminds us how hard and painful it was being a slave in Egypt. It helps us imagine soreness in our backs from lifting heavy bricks. It reminds us of the pain in our hearts when we thought we would never be free.

To understand how important freedom is, it is not enough for us to talk about slavery. Tasting the maror, we make sure we also feel at least a little bit of the slaves' bitter pain. It helps us remember that when we get the choice, we choose to go free!

These three symbolic foods – the lamb bone, the matzah, and the maror – bring the feelings of the first Passover night to our own seder table. **In every generation,** no matter how long ago the first Passover night was, we try to feel that we ourselves are going free **right now.**

THANK AND PRAISE!

> While you read this paragraph, lift up your cup and make a toast to freedom!

Because of all this, we thank and praise God, who did all these miracles for our ancestors and for us.

God led us from slavery to freedom,
from despair to happiness,
from sadness to a joyful holiday,
and from darkness to a great light.

וְנֹאמַר לְפָנָיו שִׁירָה חֲדָשָׁה. הַלְלוּיָהּ.

Venomar lefanav shira chadasha. Halleluyah!

Let's sing a new song to God. Hallelujah!

We are starting to sing and celebrate!
Many more songs of thanks and praise
will come after our main meal.

When the Children of Israel marched out of Egypt, they left slavery
and felt their new strength. When we left Egypt as free people,
everything turned around. Even the sea flowed backwards, and
the Jordan River flipped. The mountains danced like leaping
rams, and the hills jumped like lambs.

Oh, Sea, how did you turn around like that?

Oh, Jordan River, how did you flow backwards?

The earth shook, and the rocks became a
pool of cool, clear water,

A fountain bubbling with joy.

בְּצֵאת יִשְׂרָאֵל מִמִּצְרָיִם, בֵּית יַעֲקֹב מֵעַם לֹעֵז. הָיְתָה יְהוּדָה לְקָדְשׁוֹ, יִשְׂרָאֵל מַמְשְׁלוֹתָיו.
הַיָּם רָאָה וַיָּנֹס, הַיַּרְדֵּן יִסֹּב לְאָחוֹר. הֶהָרִים רָקְדוּ כְאֵילִים, גְּבָעוֹת כִּבְנֵי צֹאן. מַה לְּךָ הַיָּם
כִּי תָנוּס, הַיַּרְדֵּן תִּסֹּב לְאָחוֹר. הֶהָרִים תִּרְקְדוּ כְאֵילִים, גְּבָעוֹת כִּבְנֵי צֹאן. מִלְּפְנֵי אָדוֹן חוּלִי
אָרֶץ, מִלְּפְנֵי אֱלוֹהַּ יַעֲקֹב. הַהֹפְכִי הַצּוּר אֲגַם מָיִם, חַלָּמִישׁ לְמַעְיְנוֹ מָיִם.

Betzeit Yisra'el miMitzrayim, beit Ya'akov me'am lo'ez. Haita Yehuda
lekodsho, Yisra'el mamshelotav. Hayam ra'a vayanos, haYarden yisov
le'achor. Heharim rakdu che'eilim, geva'ot kivnei tzon.

Ma lecha hayam ki tanus	haYarden tisov le'achor.
Heharim tirkedu che'eilim	geva'ot kivnei tzon.
Milifenei adon chuli aretz	milifenei eloha Ya'akov.
Hahofchi hatzur agam mayim	chalamish lemayeno mayim.

A SPECIAL MEAL

WE'VE TOLD THE STORY!

Now we're ready to eat some of those symbolic foods on the way to our festive dinner.

SECOND CUP OF WINE

The second cup of wine or grape juice ends the storytelling part of our seder and begins our meal.

While you read these blessings, lift up your cup of wine or juice, like a toast to freedom. After you say the blessings, lean back and drink.

בָּרוּךְ אַתָּה יְיָ אֱלֹהֵינוּ מֶלֶךְ הָעוֹלָם אֲשֶׁר גְּאָלָנוּ וְגָאַל אֶת אֲבוֹתֵינוּ מִמִּצְרַיִם וְהִגִּיעָנוּ לַלַּיְלָה הַזֶּה לֶאֱכָל בּוֹ מַצָּה וּמָרוֹר. בָּרוּךְ אַתָּה יְיָ גָּאַל יִשְׂרָאֵל.

בָּרוּךְ אַתָּה יְיָ אֱלֹהֵינוּ מֶלֶךְ הָעוֹלָם בּוֹרֵא פְּרִי הַגָּפֶן.

Baruch ata Adonai, Eloheinu melech ha'olam,
asher ge'alanu vega'al et avoteinu miMitzrayim
vehigi'anu lalaila hazeh, le'echol bo matzah umaror.
Baruch ata Adonai, ga'al Yisra'el.

Baruch ata Adonai, Eloheinu melech ha'olam, borei peri hagafen.

Dear God, Creator of our world, thank You for making us and our families free, and for bringing us safely to this night, to eat matzah and maror at this seder. Dear God, thank You for making us free.

Dear God, Creator of our world, thank You for the delicious fruit that grows on vines.

Lean back in freedom and drink!

RACHTZAH, MOTZI, MATZAH
רָחְצָה, מוֹצִיא, מַצָּה
Second Hand-Washing and Blessings for Matzah

It is time to taste matzah for the first time this evening! Before we eat it, we wash our hands **(rach–TZAH)**, this time to get ready for eating our main meal. It is a tradition to say the blessing over washing our hands right before we say the **Motzi (MOE–tzee)**, the blessing for eating bread — and then, right away, the special blessing just for the first bite of matzah at the seder.

Make sure everyone gets a piece of the top matzah. Repeat the washing style from earlier in the seder on page 16 with three volunteers going around with a bowl, pitcher, and towel to wash and dry everyone's hands.

BLESSINGS FOR HAND-WASHING, THE MEAL, AND MATZAH

Hold up a bit of matzah when saying the second and third blessings.

בָּרוּךְ אַתָּה יְיָ אֱלֹהֵינוּ מֶלֶךְ הָעוֹלָם אֲשֶׁר קִדְּשָׁנוּ בְּמִצְוֹתָיו וְצִוָּנוּ עַל נְטִילַת יָדָיִם.

בָּרוּךְ אַתָּה יְיָ אֱלֹהֵינוּ מֶלֶךְ הָעוֹלָם הַמּוֹצִיא לֶחֶם מִן הָאָרֶץ.

בָּרוּךְ אַתָּה יְיָ אֱלֹהֵינוּ מֶלֶךְ הָעוֹלָם אֲשֶׁר קִדְּשָׁנוּ בְּמִצְוֹתָיו וְצִוָּנוּ עַל אֲכִילַת מַצָּה.

Baruch ata Adonai, Eloheinu melech ha'olam, asher kideshanu bemitzvotav vetzivanu al netilat yadayim.

Baruch ata Adonai, Eloheinu melech ha'olam, hamotzi lechem min ha'aretz.

Baruch ata Adonai, Eloheinu melech ha'olam, asher kideshanu bemitzvotav vetzivanu al achilat matzah.

Dear God, Creator of our world, thank You for giving us rules that make our lives special and for teaching us to wash our hands before we eat.

Dear God, Creator of our world, thank You for bringing bread out of the earth.

Dear God, Creator of our world, thank You for giving us rules that make our lives special and for teaching us to eat matzah at the seder.

When you've finished saying the blessings, lean back and take your first bite!

50

MAROR מָרוֹר
Eat the Bitter Vegetable

◇ ◦ ◈ ◦ ◈ ◦ ◈ ◦ ◈ ◦ ◇

Maror, the bitter vegetable, gives a small taste of slavery. We say a blessing over the maror, but when we eat it we do not lean to the side. For this moment, we are slaves again.

Before we eat the maror, we dip it in charoset. (See the next page for a description of charoset.) This is the "second dipping" mentioned in the Four Questions, along with the dipping of karpas (parsley) in salt water. The maror can be eaten on a piece of matzah or inside a piece of romaine lettuce.

PREPARE THE MAROR AND THEN SAY:

בָּרוּךְ אַתָּה יְיָ אֱלֹהֵינוּ מֶלֶךְ הָעוֹלָם אֲשֶׁר קִדְּשָׁנוּ בְּמִצְוֹתָיו וְצִוָּנוּ עַל אֲכִילַת מָרוֹר.

Baruch ata Adonai, Eloheinu melech ha'olam, asher kideshanu bemitzvotav vetzivanu al achilat maror.

Dear God, Creator of our world, thank You for giving us rules that make our lives special and for teaching us to eat this maror at the seder.

KORECH כּוֹרֵךְ

Eat the Matzah Sandwich

**Korech (koe–RECH)
means "make a sandwich."**
Korech brings together all of the three
foods that are symbols of the freedom
story into one spicy bite. Because these days
we no longer eat the Passover lamb, some people
put **charoset (chah–ROE–set)** in their korech.
Charoset means "clay," and it looks like the clay used
by slaves to make bricks for Pharaoh's buildings.

There are many recipes for charoset, but it is
always made from chopped fruit, spices, wine or
juice, and often nuts. Apples, cinnamon, walnuts,
and wine are common ingredients.

Give each person two small
pieces of the bottom matzah. Put a
bit of maror and charoset between
them to make a small sandwich.

Say the paragraph below and then
eat your sandwich.

Two thousand years ago, a teacher in Israel named Hillel
created one of the world's first sandwiches. Korech brings
together in a matzah sandwich bitter maror and sweet charoset.

SHULCHAN ORECH
שֻׁלְחָן עוֹרֵךְ

Eat Dinner

**Shulchan Orech (shool–CHAN oh–RECH)
means "put dinner on the table."** Enjoying the
beautiful holiday meal is another way to show we
are free. After the meal, the seder will continue.

**Put the Haggadah aside while you
enjoy the festive meal!**

TZAFUN צָפוּן

Find the Afikoman and Eat It

Tzafun (tzah-FOON) means "hidden." At the start of this seder, the adults hid the Afikoman. The meal cannot finish without this very unusual dessert – a last taste of matzah. The children have to find the Afikoman and make a deal with the adults to return the missing Afikoman. Remember, there is a prize for returning it!

The return of the Afikoman from its hiding spot means we are ready to finish our meal. At the beginning of the seder, matzah was the bread of poor slaves. Now that we are free people, with plenty of food, it is the bread of freedom and of remembering our history. With this last taste of freedom in our mouths, we are ready to say thanks for our meal and to continue the seder.

After the Afikoman is returned, divide it into pieces so everyone gets a piece to eat.

אפיקומן

> Pour a third cup of wine or grape juice. We will say the blessing for it and drink it after we say these thank-you blessings.

BARECH בָּרֵךְ

Thanks for the Meal

We thank the cooks for preparing our delicious dinner, and we thank God for creating the food we ate. **Barech (bah-RECH) means "bless,"** because the thank-you prayer we say after eating includes several blessings. It begins with an announcement section, where the leader and the rest of the seder participants call out to each other. At the end we will say the blessing and drink the third cup of wine.

שִׁיר הַמַּעֲלוֹת: בְּשׁוּב יְיָ אֶת שִׁיבַת צִיּוֹן הָיִינוּ כְּחֹלְמִים. אָז יִמָּלֵא שְׂחוֹק פִּינוּ וּלְשׁוֹנֵנוּ רִנָּה. אָז יֹאמְרוּ בַגּוֹיִם הִגְדִּיל יְיָ לַעֲשׂוֹת עִם אֵלֶּה. הִגְדִּיל יְיָ לַעֲשׂוֹת עִמָּנוּ הָיִינוּ שְׂמֵחִים. שׁוּבָה יְיָ אֶת שְׁבִיתֵנוּ כַּאֲפִיקִים בַּנֶּגֶב. הַזֹּרְעִים בְּדִמְעָה בְּרִנָּה יִקְצֹרוּ. הָלוֹךְ יֵלֵךְ וּבָכֹה נֹשֵׂא מֶשֶׁךְ הַזָּרַע בֹּא יָבֹא בְרִנָּה נֹשֵׂא אֲלֻמֹּתָיו.

Shir hama'alot: Beshuv Adonai et shivat tziyon hayinu kecholmim. Az yimalei sechok pinu ul'shoneinu rina. Az yomru vagoyim, higdil Adonai la'asot im eileh. Higdil Adonai la'asot imanu, hayinu semeichim. Shuva Adonai et sheviteinu, ka'afikim baNegev. Hazor'im bedim'a, berina yiktzoru. Haloch yelech uvacho, nosei meshech hazara, bo yavo verina, nosei alumotav.

Here is the song of a journey up to Israel: So many times in our history Jewish people were sent far away from the land of Israel. Now we are returning home, as if in a dream. Our mouths fill with laughter, and our tongues sing with joy. God has watched over the people of Israel. Come let us sing joyful songs together.

הַמְזַמֵּן: חֲבֵרַי נְבָרֵךְ!

הַמְסוּבִּין: יְהִי שֵׁם יְיָ מְבֹרָךְ מֵעַתָּה וְעַד עוֹלָם.

הַמְזַמֵּן: יְהִי שֵׁם יְיָ מְבֹרָךְ מֵעַתָּה וְעַד עוֹלָם.
בִּרְשׁוּת חֲבֵרַי, נְבָרֵךְ [אֱלֹהֵינוּ] שֶׁאָכַלְנוּ מִשֶּׁלּוֹ.

הַמְסוּבִּין: בָּרוּךְ [אֱלֹהֵינוּ] שֶׁאָכַלְנוּ מִשֶּׁלּוֹ וּבְטוּבוֹ חָיִינוּ.

הַמְזַמֵּן: בָּרוּךְ [אֱלֹהֵינוּ] שֶׁאָכַלְנוּ מִשֶּׁלּוֹ וּבְטוּבוֹ חָיִינוּ.
בָּרוּךְ הוּא וּבָרוּךְ שְׁמוֹ.

Leader: Chaverai, nevarech!

Group: Yehi shem Adonai mevorach me'ata ve'ad olam.

Leader: Yehi shem Adonai mevorach me'ata ve'ad olam.
Birshut chaverai, nevarech (Eloheinu) she'achalnu mishelo.

Group: Baruch (Eloheinu) she'achalnu mishelo uvetuvo chayinu.

Leader: Baruch (Eloheinu) she'achalnu mishelo uvetuvo chayinu.
Baruch hu uvaruch shemo.

Leader: My friends, let us praise God for this meal.

Group: May God's name be blessed now and always.

Leader: Let us bless our God, who created the world and made food for us.

Group: Thank You, God, for this food we have eaten.

Leader: You give us blessings, and we bless you.

בָּרוּךְ אַתָּה יְיָ אֱלֹהֵינוּ מֶלֶךְ הָעוֹלָם הַזָּן אֶת הָעוֹלָם כֻּלּוֹ בְּטוּבוֹ בְּחֵן בְּחֶסֶד
וּבְרַחֲמִים. הוּא נוֹתֵן לֶחֶם לְכָל בָּשָׂר כִּי לְעוֹלָם חַסְדּוֹ. וּבְטוּבוֹ הַגָּדוֹל
תָּמִיד לֹא חָסַר לָנוּ וְאַל יֶחְסַר לָנוּ מָזוֹן לְעוֹלָם וָעֶד. בַּעֲבוּר
שְׁמוֹ הַגָּדוֹל כִּי הוּא אֵל זָן וּמְפַרְנֵס לַכֹּל וּמֵטִיב לַכֹּל וּמֵכִין מָזוֹן לְכָל
בְּרִיּוֹתָיו אֲשֶׁר בָּרָא. בָּרוּךְ אַתָּה יְיָ הַזָּן אֶת הַכֹּל.

Baruch ata Adonai, Eloheinu melech ha'olam, hazan et ha'olam kulo
betuvo bechen, bechesed, uv'rachamim. Hu noten lechem lechol basar
ki l'olam chasdo. Uv'tuvo hagadol, tamid lo chasar lanu, ve'al yechsar
lanu mazon l'olam va'ed. Ba'avur shemo hagadol, ki hu El zan umefarnes
lakol, umetiv lakol, umechin mazon lechol briyotav asher bara.

Baruch ata Adonai, hazan et hakol.

Dear God, Creator of our world, thank You for giving us food that makes our
bodies strong. Thank You for giving food to all with
kindness. Thank You for giving us the beautiful land of Israel, for
taking us out of Egypt, and for freeing us from slavery.
Thank You for Your Torah, which You teach us.

Thank You for everything You have given us.

עֹשֶׂה שָׁלוֹם בִּמְרוֹמָיו הוּא יַעֲשֶׂה שָׁלוֹם עָלֵינוּ וְעַל כָּל יִשְׂרָאֵל וְאִמְרוּ אָמֵן.

Oseh shalom bimromav, hu ya'aseh shalom aleinu
v'al kol Yisra'el. V'imeru: Amen.

May God, who makes peace high up in the heavens, bring peace to us, to
all the Jewish people, and to the whole world. Together we say: Amen.

THIRD CUP OF WINE

Lift up the third cup of wine or juice.
Say the blessing, and then drink while leaning.

בָּרוּךְ אַתָּה יְיָ אֱלֹהֵינוּ מֶלֶךְ הָעוֹלָם בּוֹרֵא פְּרִי הַגָּפֶן.

Baruch ata Adonai, Eloheinu melech ha'olam, borei peri hagafen.

Dear God, Creator of our world, thank You for the delicious fruit
that grows on vines.

WE'RE FREE. LET'S CELEBRATE!

We escaped from Pharaoh, told our story, and enjoyed our Passover meal. Now it's time to celebrate our freedom!

First, we stop to hope for a future when the whole world will be free. Then we sing songs of praise and celebration.

ELIJAH'S CUP

אליהו

Why do some people force other people to be slaves? Why do some people have hard lives while others get to be free? Why did Egyptians have to suffer when the Jews were being saved?

In many Jewish stories, a special man named Elijah the Prophet helps us dream of a happier and fairer world. On Passover, Elijah has a special job: he travels around the world to visit every seder, reminding us to have hope and keep working for fairness and justice.

We welcome Elijah with a special cup of wine, just for him.

Have everyone pour a bit of wine or juice into Elijah's cup. Then stand up from the table and open the front door to welcome Elijah.

Smell the nighttime air. Listen to the sounds of evening. Where is Elijah? Will he visit our seder and have a drink with us? Did he already sip from his cup?

Earlier tonight we asked:
Ma Nishtana?
What is different?

Now we can ask:
How can we help make
a difference?

Can we make our world a place
where Elijah would want to stay?

Together we sing a song for
Elijah that hopes for a day
when everyone will be free.

אֵלִיָּהוּ הַנָּבִיא, אֵלִיָּהוּ הַתִּשְׁבִּי, אֵלִיָּהוּ הַגִּלְעָדִי
בִּמְהֵרָה בְּיָמֵינוּ יָבוֹא אֵלֵינוּ עִם מָשִׁיחַ בֶּן דָּוִד.

**Eliyahu hanavi, Eliyahu hatishbi, Eliyahu hagil'adi
Bimhera b'yameinu yavo eleinu im mashiach ben David.**

Elijah the Prophet, Elijah from Tishbi, Elijah from Gilad
Come soon to us, bringing a time of peace for the world.

MIRIAM'S CUP

The Jewish people would not have gone free from Egypt without the actions of many brave women. Moses' mother Yocheved and his older sister Miriam hid baby Moses in a basket on the Nile River. The Egyptian princess who found little Moses kept him safe in the palace. Shifra and Puah were midwives who also saved Jewish babies.

After the Jewish people escaped through the Sea of Reeds, Miriam led them in song. The tradition is that wherever Miriam traveled in the desert, a well of refreshing water would appear. Miriam's music and pools of water kept the Jewish people strong on their long journey through the desert to Israel.

AS WE FILL MIRIAM'S CUP and take a sip from our own glass of water, we remember Miriam and the many women who helped keep the Jewish people strong and safe.

Have everyone pour a bit of water into Miriam's cup, and then take a sip from their own glass.

Pour the fourth cup of wine or grape juice to get it ready to drink after Hallel.

HALLEL הַלֵּל

Singing Praise and Freedom Songs

Hallel means "praise." The English word "Hallelujah!" is related to "hallel" and means "Praise God!" Before our meal we sang thanks to God for having saved us from slavery in Egypt, and now we sing about hope for the future.

DO YOU KNOW MORE SONGS of praise or gratitude (maybe with the word "Hallelujah") or songs about freedom? The songs can be in any language. Now is the time to sing them!

הוֹדוּ לַיְיָ כִּי טוֹב   כִּי לְעוֹלָם חַסְדּוֹ.

יֹאמַר נָא יִשְׂרָאֵל   כִּי לְעוֹלָם חַסְדּוֹ.

יֹאמְרוּ נָא בֵית אַהֲרֹן   כִּי לְעוֹלָם חַסְדּוֹ.

יֹאמְרוּ נָא יִרְאֵי יְיָ   כִּי לְעוֹלָם חַסְדּוֹ.

Hodu l'Adonai ki tov, ki l'olam chasdo.

Yomar na Yisra'el, ki l'olam chasdo.

Yomru na veit Aharon, ki l'olam chasdo.

Yomru na yir'ei Adonai, ki l'olam chasdo.

Let's thank God, who is good. God's kindness lasts forever.

Let the family of Israel say: God's kindness lasts forever.

Let the family of Aaron say: God's kindness lasts forever.

Let God's followers say: God's kindness lasts forever.

FOURTH CUP OF WINE

Lift up the fourth cup of wine or grape juice, say the blessing, and then drink while leaning.

בָּרוּךְ אַתָּה יְיָ אֱלֹהֵינוּ מֶלֶךְ הָעוֹלָם
בּוֹרֵא פְּרִי הַגָּפֶן.

Baruch ata Adonai, Eloheinu melech ha'olam, borei peri hagafen.

Dear God, Creator of our world, thank You for the delicious fruit that grows on vines.

NIRTZAH נִרְצָה

The End

This last part of our seder is called **Nirtzah (near-TZAH)**, a quick way to say: "Our seder is ending and we hope God accepts our thanks." We celebrate the end of the seder with a few classic Passover songs.

We did it! Let's sing!

ADIR HU

אַדִּיר הוּא

God Is Strong

Adir Hu means "God is strong." In Hebrew, each line of the song begins with a different letter of the alphabet. Each letter starts a word that describes one of God's qualities: strong, wise, and caring. We hope to act in these kind ways, too.

אַדִּיר הוּא יִבְנֶה בֵיתוֹ בְּקָרוֹב, בִּמְהֵרָה בְּיָמֵינוּ בְּקָרוֹב. אֵל בְּנֵה, בְּנֵה בֵיתְךָ בְּקָרוֹב.

בָּחוּר הוּא, גָּדוֹל הוּא, דָּגוּל הוּא, יִבְנֶה בֵיתוֹ בְּקָרוֹב...

הָדוּר הוּא, וָתִיק הוּא, זַכַּאי הוּא, חָסִיד הוּא, יִבְנֶה בֵיתוֹ בְּקָרוֹב...

טָהוֹר הוּא, יָחִיד הוּא, כַּבִּיר הוּא, לָמוּד הוּא, מֶלֶךְ הוּא, נוֹרָא הוּא,

סַגִּיב הוּא, עִזּוּז הוּא, פּוֹדֶה הוּא, צַדִּיק הוּא, יִבְנֶה בֵיתוֹ בְּקָרוֹב...

קָדוֹשׁ הוּא, רַחוּם הוּא, שַׁדַּי הוּא, תַּקִּיף הוּא, יִבְנֶה בֵיתוֹ בְּקָרוֹב...

God is strong!

God, make a place for Yourself soon.

Build it, build it —
make Your special place soon!

Adir hu, yivneh veito bekarov, bimhera b'yameinu bekarov.

El benei, benei veitcha bekarov.

Bachur hu, gadol hu, dagul hu, yivneh veito bekarov,
bimhera b'yameinu bekarov.

El benei, benei veitcha bekarov.

Hadur hu, vatik hu, zakai hu, chasid hu, yivneh veito
bekarov, bimhera b'yameinu bekarov.

El benei, benei veitcha bekarov.

Tahor hu, yachid hu, kabir hu, lamud hu, melech hu, nora hu,
sagiv hu, izuz hu, podeh hu, tzadik hu, yivneh veito bekarov,
bimhera b'yameinu bekarov.

El benei, benei veitcha bekarov.

Kadosh hu, rachum hu, shadai hu, takif hu, yivneh veito
bekarov, bimhera b'yameinu bekarov.

El benei, benei veitcha bekarov.

ECHAD MI YODE'A
אֶחָד מִי יוֹדֵעַ?
Who Knows One?

Just as "Adir Hu" goes in order of the letters, "Echad Mi Yode'a" goes in order of the numbers. With each number, the song asks a question: "Who knows what this number means?" The answer each time is something Jewish. Sing along and have fun! Transliteration is on page 72.

אֶחָד מִי יוֹדֵעַ? אֶחָד אֲנִי יוֹדֵעַ: אֶחָד אֱלֹהֵינוּ שֶׁבַּשָּׁמַיִם וּבָאָרֶץ.

שְׁנַיִם מִי יוֹדֵעַ? שְׁנַיִם אֲנִי יוֹדֵעַ: שְׁנֵי לֻחוֹת הַבְּרִית, אֶחָד אֱלֹהֵינוּ שֶׁבַּשָּׁמַיִם וּבָאָרֶץ.

שְׁלֹשָׁה מִי יוֹדֵעַ? שְׁלֹשָׁה אֲנִי יוֹדֵעַ: שְׁלֹשָׁה אָבוֹת, שְׁנֵי לֻחוֹת הַבְּרִית, אֶחָד אֱלֹהֵינוּ שֶׁבַּשָּׁמַיִם וּבָאָרֶץ.

אַרְבַּע מִי יוֹדֵעַ? אַרְבַּע אֲנִי יוֹדֵעַ: אַרְבַּע אִמָּהוֹת, שְׁלֹשָׁה...

חֲמִשָּׁה מִי יוֹדֵעַ? חֲמִשָּׁה אֲנִי יוֹדֵעַ: חֲמִשָּׁה חוּמְשֵׁי תּוֹרָה, אַרְבַּע...

שִׁשָּׁה מִי יוֹדֵעַ? שִׁשָּׁה אֲנִי יוֹדֵעַ: שִׁשָּׁה סִדְרֵי מִשְׁנָה, חֲמִשָּׁה...

שִׁבְעָה מִי יוֹדֵעַ? שִׁבְעָה אֲנִי יוֹדֵעַ: שִׁבְעָה יְמֵי שַׁבְּתָּא, שִׁשָּׁה...

שְׁמוֹנָה מִי יוֹדֵעַ? שְׁמוֹנָה אֲנִי יוֹדֵעַ: שְׁמוֹנָה יְמֵי מִילָה, שִׁבְעָה...

תִּשְׁעָה מִי יוֹדֵעַ? תִּשְׁעָה אֲנִי יוֹדֵעַ: תִּשְׁעָה יַרְחֵי לֵדָה, שְׁמוֹנָה...

עֲשָׂרָה מִי יוֹדֵעַ? עֲשָׂרָה אֲנִי יוֹדֵעַ: עֲשָׂרָה דִבְּרַיָּא, תִּשְׁעָה...

אַחַד עָשָׂר מִי יוֹדֵעַ? אַחַד עָשָׂר אֲנִי יוֹדֵעַ: אַחַד עָשָׂר כּוֹכְבַיָּא, עֲשָׂרָה...

שְׁנֵים עָשָׂר מִי יוֹדֵעַ? שְׁנֵים עָשָׂר אֲנִי יוֹדֵעַ: שְׁנֵים עָשָׂר שִׁבְטַיָּא, אַחַד עָשָׂר...

שְׁלֹשָׁה עָשָׂר מִי יוֹדֵעַ? שְׁלֹשָׁה עָשָׂר אֲנִי יוֹדֵעַ: שְׁלֹשָׁה עָשָׂר מִדַּיָּא, שְׁנֵים עָשָׂר שִׁבְטַיָּא, אַחַד עָשָׂר כּוֹכְבַיָּא, עֲשָׂרָה דִבְּרַיָּא, תִּשְׁעָה יַרְחֵי לֵדָה, שְׁמוֹנָה יְמֵי מִילָה, שִׁבְעָה יְמֵי שַׁבְּתָּא, שִׁשָּׁה סִדְרֵי מִשְׁנָה, חֲמִשָּׁה חוּמְשֵׁי תּוֹרָה, אַרְבַּע אִמָּהוֹת, שְׁלֹשָׁה אָבוֹת, שְׁנֵי לֻחוֹת הַבְּרִית, אֶחָד אֱלֹהֵינוּ שֶׁבַּשָּׁמַיִם וּבָאָרֶץ.

Who knows 1? I know 1! 1 is our God – in heaven and on earth!

Who knows 2? I know 2! 2 are the tablets from Mount Sinai. 1 is our God – in heaven and on earth!

Who knows 3? I know 3! 3 are the founding Fathers [of the Jewish people]. 2 are the tablets from Mount Sinai. 1 is our God – in heaven and on earth!

Who knows 4? I know 4! 4 are the founding Mothers [of the Jewish people]. 3 are...

Who knows 5? I know 5! 5 are the books of the Torah. 4 are...

Who knows 6? I know 6! 6 are the books of the Mishnah. 5 are...

Who knows 7? I know 7! 7 are the days of the week. 6 are....

Who knows 8? I know 8! 8 are the days until *brit milah* (circumcision). 7 are...

Who knows 9? I know 9! 9 are the months until a baby is born. 8 are...

Who knows 10? I know 10! 10 are the Ten Commandments. 9 are...

Who knows 11? I know 11! 11 are the stars in Joseph's dream. 10 are...

Who knows 12? I know 12! 12 are the tribes of Israel. 11 are...

Who knows 13? I know 13! 13 are God's special qualities. 12 are the tribes of Israel. 11 are the stars in Joseph's dream. 10 are the Ten Commandments. 9 are the months until a baby is born. 8 are the days until *brit milah* (circumcision). 7 are the days of the week. 6 are the books of the Mishnah. 5 are the books of the Torah. 4 are the founding Mothers. 3 are the founding Fathers. 2 are the tablets from Mount Sinai, and 1 is our God – in heaven and on earth!

Echad mi yode'a? Echad ani yode'a: echad Eloheinu, shebashamayim uva'aretz.

Shnayim mi yode'a? Shnayim ani yode'a: shnei luchot habrit, echad Eloheinu, shebashamayim uva'aretz.

Shlosha mi yode'a? Shlosha ani yode'a: shlosha avot, shnei luchot habrit, echad Eloheinu, shebashamayim uva'aretz.

Arba mi yode'a? Arba ani yode'a: arba imahot, shlosha avot, shnei luchot habrit, echad Eloheinu, shebashamayim uva'aretz.

Chamisha mi yode'a? Chamisha ani yode'a: chamisha chumshei Torah, arba imahot, shlosha avot, shnei luchot habrit, echad Eloheinu, shebashamayim uva'aretz.

Shisha mi yode'a? Shisha ani yode'a: shisha sidrei Mishnah, chamisha chumshei Torah, arba imahot, shlosha avot, shnei luchot habrit, echad Eloheinu, shebashamayim uva'aretz.

Shiv'a mi yode'a? Shiv'a ani yode'a: shiv'a yemei shabata, shisha sidrei Mishnah, chamisha chumshei Torah, arba imahot, shlosha avot, shnei luchot habrit, echad Eloheinu, shebashamayim uva'aretz.

8

Shmona mi yode'a? Shmona ani yode'a: shmona yemei milah, shiv'a yemei shabata, shisha sidrei Mishnah, chamisha chumshei Torah, arba imahot, shlosha avot, shnei luchot habrit, echad Eloheinu, shebashamayim uva'aretz.

9

Tish'a mi yode'a? Tish'a ani yode'a: tish'a yarchei leida, shmona yemei milah, shiv'a yemei shabata, shisha sidrei Mishnah, chamisha chumshei Torah, arba imahot, shlosha avot, shnei luchot habrit, echad Eloheinu, shebashamayim uva'aretz.

10

Asara mi yode'a? Asara ani yode'a: asara dibraya, tish'a yarchei leida, shmona yemei milah, shiv'a yemei shabata, shisha sidrei Mishnah, chamisha chumshei Torah, arba imahot, shlosha avot, shnei luchot habrit, echad Eloheinu, shebashamayim uva'aretz.

11

Achad asar mi yode'a? Achad asar ani yode'a: achad asar kochvaya, asara dibraya, tish'a yarchei leida, shmona yemei milah, shiv'a yemei shabata, shisha sidrei Mishnah, chamisha chumshei Torah, arba imahot, shlosha avot, shnei luchot habrit, echad Eloheinu, shebashamayim uva'aretz.

12

Shneim asar mi yode'a? Shneim asar ani yode'a: shneim asar shivtaya, achad asar kochvaya, asara dibraya, tish'a yarchei leida, shmona yemei milah, shiv'a yemei shabata, shisha sidrei Mishnah, chamisha chumshei Torah, arba imahot, shlosha avot, shnei luchot habrit, echad Eloheinu, shebashamayim uva'aretz.

13

Shlosha asar mi yode'a? Shlosha asar ani yode'a: shlosha asar midaya, shneim asar shivtaya, achad asar kochvaya, asara dibraya, tish'a yarchei leida, shmona yemei milah, shiv'a yemei shabata, shisha sidrei Mishnah, chamisha chumshei Torah, arba imahot, shlosha avot, shnei luchot habrit, echad Eloheinu, shebashamayim uva'aretz.

CHAD GADYA

חַד גַּדְיָא

Just One Little Goat

This Haggadah has one last song. It's also a game: a long chase, with one verse after another describing someone chased by someone else stronger, until in the end only God's power remains. Translation and transliteration on pages 76 and 77.

Let each person at the table choose one character or object from the story and make its noise every time its name comes around while everyone else sings. Your table will get noisier and more dramatic as the verses get longer!

דְּזַבִּין אַבָּא בִּתְרֵי זוּזֵי, חַד גַּדְיָא, חַד גַּדְיָא.

וְאָתָא שׁוּנְרָא וְאָכְלָה לְגַדְיָא, דְּזַבִּין אַבָּא בִּתְרֵי זוּזֵי, חַד גַּדְיָא, חַד גַּדְיָא.

וְאָתָא כַלְבָּא וְנָשַׁךְ לְשׁוּנְרָא, דְּאָכְלָה לְגַדְיָא, דְּזַבִּין אַבָּא בִּתְרֵי זוּזֵי, חַד גַּדְיָא, חַד גַּדְיָא.

וְאָתָא חוּטְרָא וְהִכָּה לְכַלְבָּא, דְּנָשַׁךְ לְשׁוּנְרָא, דְּאָכְלָה לְגַדְיָא, דְּזַבִּין אַבָּא בִּתְרֵי זוּזֵי, חַד גַּדְיָא, חַד גַּדְיָא.

וְאָתָא נוּרָא וְשָׂרַף לְחוּטְרָא, דְּהִכָּה לְכַלְבָּא, דְּנָשַׁךְ לְשׁוּנְרָא, דְּאָכְלָה לְגַדְיָא, דְּזַבִּין אַבָּא בִּתְרֵי זוּזֵי, חַד גַּדְיָא, חַד גַּדְיָא.

וְאָתָא מַיָּא וְכָבָה לְנוּרָא, דְּשָׂרַף לְחוּטְרָא, דְּהִכָּה לְכַלְבָּא, דְּנָשַׁךְ לְשׁוּנְרָא, דְּאָכְלָה לְגַדְיָא, דְּזַבִּין אַבָּא בִּתְרֵי זוּזֵי, חַד גַּדְיָא, חַד גַּדְיָא.

וְאָתָא תוֹרָא וְשָׁתָא לְמַיָּא, דְּכָבָה לְנוּרָא, דְּשָׂרַף לְחוּטְרָא, דְּהִכָּה לְכַלְבָּא, דְּנָשַׁךְ לְשׁוּנְרָא, דְּאָכְלָה לְגַדְיָא, דְּזַבִּין אַבָּא בִּתְרֵי זוּזֵי, חַד גַּדְיָא, חַד גַּדְיָא.

וְאָתָא הַשּׁוֹחֵט וְשָׁחַט לְתוֹרָא, דְּשָׁתָא לְמַיָּא, דְּכָבָה לְנוּרָא, דְּשָׂרַף לְחוּטְרָא, דְּהִכָּה לְכַלְבָּא, דְּנָשַׁךְ לְשׁוּנְרָא, דְּאָכְלָה לְגַדְיָא, דְּזַבִּין אַבָּא בִּתְרֵי זוּזֵי, חַד גַּדְיָא, חַד גַּדְיָא.

וְאָתָא מַלְאַךְ הַמָּוֶת וְשָׁחַט לְשׁוֹחֵט, דְּשָׁחַט לְתוֹרָא, דְּשָׁתָא לְמַיָּא, דְּכָבָה לְנוּרָא, דְּשָׂרַף לְחוּטְרָא, דְּהִכָּה לְכַלְבָּא, דְּנָשַׁךְ לְשׁוּנְרָא, דְּאָכְלָה לְגַדְיָא, דְּזַבִּין אַבָּא בִּתְרֵי זוּזֵי, חַד גַּדְיָא, חַד גַּדְיָא.

וְאָתָא הַקָּדוֹשׁ בָּרוּךְ הוּא וְשָׁחַט לְמַלְאַךְ הַמָּוֶת, דְּשָׁחַט לְשׁוֹחֵט, דְּשָׁחַט לְתוֹרָא, דְּשָׁתָא לְמַיָּא, דְּכָבָה לְנוּרָא, דְּשָׂרַף לְחוּטְרָא, דְּהִכָּה לְכַלְבָּא, דְּנָשַׁךְ לְשׁוּנְרָא, דְּאָכְלָה לְגַדְיָא, דְּזַבִּין אַבָּא בִּתְרֵי זוּזֵי, חַד גַּדְיָא, חַד גַּדְיָא.

Dezabin abba bitrei zuzei.
Chad gadya, chad gadya!

Va'ata shunra v'achla legadya dezabin abba bitrei zuzei.
Chad gadya, chad gadya!

Va'ata chalba venashach leshunra, d'achla legadya
dezabin abba bitrei zuzei. **Chad gadya, chad gadya!**

Va'ata chutra vehika lechalba, denashach leshunra, d'achla legadya
dezabin abba bitrei zuzei. **Chad gadya, chad gadya!**

Va'ata nura vesaraf lechutra, dehika lechalba, denashach leshunra,
d'achla legadya dezabin abba bitrei zuzei. **Chad gadya, chad gadya!**

Va'ata maya vechava lenura, desaraf lechutra, dehika lechalba,
denashach leshunra, d'achla legadya dezabin abba bitrei zuzei.
Chad gadya, chad gadya!

Va'ata tora veshata lemaya, dechava lenura, desaraf lechutra, dehika
lechalba, denashach leshunra, d'achla legadya dezabin abba bitrei
zuzei. **Chad gadya, chad gadya!**

Va'ata hashochet veshachat letora, deshata lemaya, dechava lenura,
desaraf lechutra, dehika lechalba, denashach leshunra, d'achla legadya
dezabin abba bitrei zuzei. **Chad gadya, chad gadya!**

Va'ata malach hamavet veshachat leshochet, deshachat letora,
deshata lemaya, dechava lenura, desaraf lechutra,
dehika lechalba, denashach leshunra, d'achla legadya
dezabin abba bitrei zuzei. **Chad gadya, chad gadya!**

Va'ata haKadosh Baruch Hu veshachat lemalach hamavet, deshachat
leshochet, deshachat letora, deshata lemaya, dechava lenura, desaraf
lechutra, dehika lechalba, denashach leshunra, d'achla legadya
dezabin abba bitrei zuzei. **Chad gadya, chad gadya!**

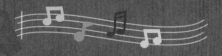

My father bought it for just two coins.
One little goat, one little goat!

Then the cat came and ate the goat that my father bought for just two coins. **One little goat, one little goat!**

Then the dog came and bit the cat that ate the goat that my father bought for just two coins. **One little goat, one little goat!**

Then the stick came and hit the dog that bit the cat that ate the goat that my father bought for just two coins. **One little goat, one little goat!**

Then the fire came and burned the stick that hit the dog that bit the cat that ate the goat that my father bought for just two coins. **One little goat, one little goat!**

Then the water came and put out the fire that burned the stick that hit the dog that bit the cat that ate the goat that my father bought for just two coins. **One little goat, one little goat!**

Then the ox came and drank the water that put out the fire that burned the stick that hit the dog that bit the cat that ate the goat that my father bought for just two coins. **One little goat, one little goat!**

Then the butcher came and slaughtered the ox that drank the water that put out the fire that burned the stick that hit the dog that bit the cat that ate the goat that my father bought for just two coins. **One little goat, one little goat!**

Then the Angel of Death came and killed the butcher that slaughtered the ox that drank the water that put out the fire that burned the stick that hit the dog that bit the cat that ate the goat that my father bought for just two coins. **One little goat, one little goat!**

Then God came and defeated the Angel of Death that killed the butcher that slaughtered the ox that drank the water that put out the fire that burned the stick that hit the dog that bit the cat that ate the goat that my father bought for just two coins. **One little goat, one little goat!**

NEXT YEAR IN
JERUSALEM

EVERYONE READS TOGETHER:

We began the seder as slaves tasting salty tears. Then we raced through the desert sand and ate matzah baked in a hurry. We passed through the Sea of Reeds and escaped from Pharaoh's army. We praised God for helping us escape and saving our lives.

Our job of remembering and re-living this amazing adventure is now complete. We have finished our seder and told our story of freedom.

We now move from the past to the future.
How will I grow this year? How will the world change? How can we keep moving from slavery to freedom?

THE HAGGADAH ENDS WITH GREAT
HOPE FOR THE FUTURE:

לְשָׁנָה הַבָּאָה בִּירוּשָׁלָיִם!

Leshana haba'a biYerushalayim!

Next year in Jerusalem!
Next year may all people be free!

79

> # IN EVERY GENERATION WE SHOULD SEE OURSELVES AS IF WE PERSONALLY CAME OUT OF EGYPT.

Shalom! Because this book has Hebrew, which is read from right to left, we start at the other end. Flip to the other side to get started.